Hello, my name is St. Kateri Tekakwitha!

Dedicated To:
Camp Tekakwitha

Written By: Abigail Gartland

I was born in the Mohawk Village in the year 1656.

When I was a little girl, I became very sick with small pox, which left many scars

My whole family got sick, and I was the nly one who survived.

I was very, very sad, but I knew that Jesus was always there to comfort me.

I prayed to Jesus every day.

When I was 19 years old, I became a Catholic.

That means, I was not baptized Catholic as a baby. As I grew up, I put my trust in Jesus and found truth with God.

I loved serving my community and teaching others about the love of Jesus.

After years of serving others and dedicating my life to Jesus, I went to be with Him in Heaven on April 17, 1680.

I went to Heaven to spend eternity with Jesus.

Do you want to be more like me?

You can celebrate my feast day with me on July 14th.

I am the patron saint of nature and the environment!

I pray for you every day of your life.

St. Kateri Tekakwitha, Pray for us!

Copyright:

Clipart: 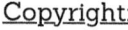 © PentoolPixie © LimeandKiwiDesigns
Licensed purchased: 1/10/2024

About the Author

Abigail Gartland

I love the saints and I love my faith. The idea for sharing the stories of the saints with little ones came when my dear friends were expecting their first baby. I wanted to create something as unique and special as our friendship. Each book is dedicated to very special people and groups who have enriched my faith in different ways. I am blessed to write these stories and appreciate the unending support of my family and friends. When I am not writing, I am a middle school teacher. I hope you enjoy these stories. I pray for each and every person who opens one of my books to learn more about the saints.

Abbie

www.ingramcontent.com/pod-product-compliance
Lightning Source LLC
LaVergne TN
LVHW050134080526
838201LV00120B/4911